journey

Gonna take a sentimental journey
Gonna set my heart at ease
Gonna make a sentimental journey
To renew old memories

I got my bag, I got my reservation
Spent each dime I could afford
Like a child in wild anticipation
I long to hear that: "All aboard!"

Images from the Golden Age of Rail Travel

ABOARD!

Lynn Johnson and Michael O'Leary

CHRONICLE BOOKS
SAN FRANCISCO

ACKNOWLEDGMENTS

All Aboard! required the talent and support of many people, including Dori, Carrie, Janice, Erlyn, Les, Sandra, and King Monty.

Scott Bloom generously supplied many images from his vast collection of rail-related material and added his own genius in the darkroom, taking often crumbling paper items and transferring them to film.

Editor Alan E. Rapp helped smooth over all the usual, and unusual, problems that are a part of the creation of any book.

Printed in Hong Kong
Designed by Laura Lovett
Typeset in Jason and Trafton Script, created by Dan Solo; Bodega Sans Light and Dax Condensed by FontHaus.

Distributed in Canada by Raincoast Books
8680 Cambie Street
Vancouver, British Columbia V6P 6M9

10 9 8 7 6 5 4 3 2 1

Chronicle Books
85 Second Street
San Francisco, California 94105

www.chroniclebooks.com

Library of Congress Cataloging-in-Publication Data
Johnson, Lynn.
    All aboard! : images from the golden age of rail travel / Lynn Johnson and Michael O'Leary.
    132 p.   22.2 x 20.3 cm.
    ISBN 0-8118-1747-4
    1. Advertising—Railroads—United States. 2. Commercial art—United States. I. O'Leary, Michael (Michael D.) II. Title.
    NC1002.R34J65   1999
    741.6'7—dc21   98-49718
                                             CIP

Half title page: "Sentimental Journey." Words and music by Bud Green, Les Brown, and Ben Homer, copyright © 1944 (Renewed) Morley Music Co. All rights reserved.

Photographs on pages 8–9, 10–11, and 48 courtesy of Burlington Northern Santa Fe Railway.

Photograph on page 41 courtesy of Corbis/Bettmann-UPI.

Photograph on page 81 courtesy of Corbis/Bettmann-Gendreau.

CONTENTS

INTRODUCTION

The sound of a steam whistle blasting from a locomotive roaring

through the nighttime countryside is deeply etched upon the

American memory. The twentieth century has seen the

rise and decline of the golden age of rail travel, a

time when the majority of the traveling

American public went

by rail.

DURING

this period, the rapid development of the locomotive and its associated cars also created a comfortable, relatively fast, and often luxurious method of mass transportation.

With the advent of the sleekly styled streamliner, the imagination of the American public was captured with a new image of train travel being glamorous. Hollywood quickly caught on to this trend and began producing films such as *The Lady Vanishes, Rome Express, Secret Agent, Last Train from Madrid, Ministry of Fear,* and *Narrow Margin* that all helped advance the concept of the train as a glamorous and often exotic way to travel.

The streamliner seemed to point the way out of the Great Depression, its silver sides thrusting forward to what was hoped to be a brighter future.

Trains helped colonize the western United States; but quickly following settlement, they also began to haul increasingly large numbers of tourists to view the region's magnificent natural sights.

During World War II, trains contributed significantly to the national war effort, hauling the majority of supplies, cargo, and troops to ports for transfer to the fighting fronts and final victory over the Axis powers.

After the war, a new generation of trains was created to lure the newly emerging middle class, which had the time and money for travel. However, the railroads did not count on the rapid development of the airliner

nor the building of the efficient system of interstate highways that allowed automobiles to cross the country rapidly and freely.

The great passenger trains could no longer compete, and by the late 1950s many of the once-famous trains had been withdrawn from service and sold abroad or scrapped.

In *All Aboard!,* we examine some of the graphic images utilized to promote and advertise rail travel during the twentieth century. These images comprise every form of art movement popular during the period, while also illustrating the transition of American lifestyles.

We have also included a chapter to show similar art in Britain and Europe that, while presenting basically the same message, utilized a much different graphic style.

As we prepare to enter the twenty-first century, it is of interest to note the gradual rise in passenger train travel. Trains are once again coming into favor; passengers are being offered a chance to see the country in a relaxed manner with excellent service, a far cry from the cramped seats and minimal service that now characterizes the airlines. Also, in Britain and Europe, the famed Orient Express has returned to create an ultra-deluxe service that offers travelers the excitement and adventure that harks back to the golden age of the rails.

photograph, 1934 ▲

The *Pioneer Zephyr*, the first of
Burlington Route's *Zephyr* trains,
went into service on April 18,
1934. The *Zephyr's* observation
car featured art deco furnishings
typical of the period.

BY 1900, an incredible 90 percent of the rail lines that exist today were already in place, giving an idea of how much the steel rails had become an essential part of American life. Most historians agree that the United States' pioneering period ended

"LET'S TAKE THE TRAIN!"

How advertising art helped railroads capture passengers during the golden days of American rail travel

in approximately 1890 and that, after that point, the nation moved into a protracted settling of the vast areas of the west and northwest. However, the first three decades of the new century held great change—ranging from early isolationism to entry into the Great War to the booming Roaring Twenties to the gray pall of the Great Depression.

Before 1900, train travel was often the province of the wealthy; but, with the turn of the century, the rails became the property of everyone, and it was during this period that the train whistle became a part of the fabric of American life.

Rail advertising kept pace with the increasing passenger traffic. Ads from the early part of the century show well-dressed patrons enjoying the scenery from the open rear decks of the observation cars. This rather interesting way of encountering nature disappeared as the speed of the trains increased with the introduction of new locomotives, causing such viewing platforms to be not only uncomfortable but also dangerous. With the increase in speed, came advertising promoting the efficiency of the train, especially on cross-country runs.

With the collapse of the stock market and the onset of the Great Depression, passenger traffic fell dramatically. By 1931, passenger trains were averaging only forty-three passengers per run. Oddly, the downward trend was reversed with the introduction of the streamliner. The streamliner—of which both engines and cars had a futuristic aerodynamic design—personified glamour and a sense of accomplishment; the train actually gave the impression of propelling the United States out of the Depression. Heavy advertising emphasized the streamliner's speed, smooth ride, and elegant service. Often sold out weeks ahead, these trains were soon earning over $5.00 per mile, compared to just $1.50 per mile for the "average" passenger train.

World War II brought a whole different style of passenger rail travel. During the war, with gas rationing and a shortage of rubber for tires, Americans were often forced to take the train instead of using their autos, but they had to fight for seats with passengers given priority access by the military and government. With the end of the war, railroads brought out a new generation of fast and comfortable trains that were able to handle what they thought would be a deluge of new customers. In 1941, the railroads operated a whopping five times as many route miles as the

magazine covers, ▶
1933–1945
America's fascination with the rails coincided with the golden age of pulp magazines, which were packed with stories, mainly fiction, of life and adventure on the rails.

airlines. However, World War II had redefined air travel, and by the late 1940s fast, reliable, and comfortable airliners were available in quantity from companies like Lockheed and Boeing. Also, railroad prices were skyrocketing, and most lines were actually losing money on their deluxe dining services. Companies expanded their train schedules and promoted a future where 100-mile-per-hour trains would be standard. Performance did improve. For example, the 1940 Santa Fe *Chief,* on its Chicago to Los Angeles run, took just over sixty-eight hours, while the 1946 *Super Chief* did the same in just under forty hours. National advertising extolled the comfort and speed of these new trains.

To illustrate just how rapidly rail's passenger reversals were taking place note that, in 1946, the trains were hauling about 90 percent of the first-class business. By 1949, that figure was down to 60 percent, and airline growth would make it 50 percent in the next year. Likewise, nearly every returning serviceman wanted his own auto and the freedom that the vehicle would bring. Car sales skyrocketed and the government began laying plans for a high-speed interstate highway system.

Between the cars and the planes, the railroads began intensive advertising cam-

paigns, with emphasis on the "new, improved" service they would be giving the traveler—even in coach. Americans began to take more vacations, and the railroads appealed to them by stressing that the rails could get them to their destinations comfortably, economically, and efficiently.

However, the writing was on the wall by the end of the 1950s; the expansion of aircraft and automobile travel had ended the golden age of the passenger train. On the following pages is just a fraction of the alluring art that encapsulated a time in American life when just about everyone said, "Let's take the train!"

▲ **label, 1938**

Baltimore & Ohio promoted their service to the nation's capital by using art that combined the train and the Capitol building.

◀ **timetable, 1910**

A rather romantic scene of rail travel forms the cover for this Baltimore & Ohio time schedule. These open-ended observation cars were extremely popular, but their use came to an end as trains began to achieve higher and higher track speeds.

advertisement, 1910 ▶
Southern Pacific's water and rail route linked the West Coast with New York, as illustrated in this evocative painting.

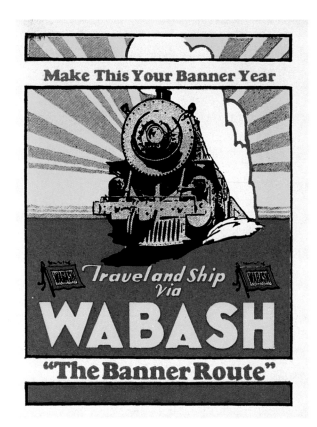

baggage label, c. 1945 ▲
▲ baggage label, 1927

This 1920s Wabash baggage label urged the user both to travel and to ship goods on the railroad. The 1940s-era label above encourages post-World War II passenger and cargo business.

advertising art, 1950 ▶

This powerful image of a speeding streamliner highlights the rail artist's preference for depicting technology intruding into remote natural locales.

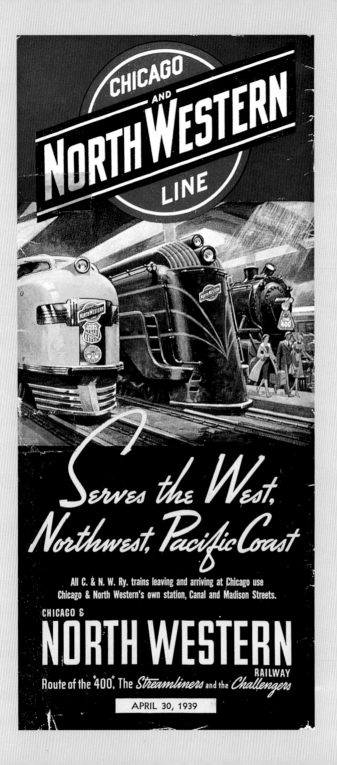

timetables, ◀ 1939, 1955 ▶

Timetables often used attractive paintings, dynamic photographs, or stylized art of line equipment to help passengers form a feeling of affiliation with the companies and their services. Three generations of North Western locomotives are illustrated on the cover of a 1939 timetable for the line that "Serves the West, Northwest, Pacific Coast." Two 1955 tables from Union Pacific promote service on the Streamliner *City of Denver* and Domeliner *City of Los Angeles* with appropriate illustrations of the equipment.

Domeliner
"CITY OF LOS ANGELES"
DAILY BETWEEN
CHICAGO · LOS ANGELES

UNION PACIFIC RAILROAD

Streamliner
"City of Denver"
between
CHICAGO and **DENVER**

UNION PACIFIC RAILROAD

OVERNIGHT.. EVERY NIGHT

◀ timetable, 1928
baggage labels, 1904–47 ▶

North Western/Union Pacific/Southern
Pacific's *Challenger* service offered
an on-board nurse, who was proudly
illustrated on their timetables and
baggage labels (1928). This was
probably done as a counter to the
early airlines, whose first stewardesses
also had to be registered nurses.

Missouri Pacific labels used starburst
and rail motifs to promote the 1904
World's Fair. Like other rail companies,
they also used dramatic slogans in
their advertising, such as this foil-
stamped label for the "Route of the
Eagles" (1938).

The Chesapeake and Ohio Lines utilized a very effective advertising tool
in the form of "America's Sleepheart"—
a logo comprising a sleeping kitten
within a heart (1947).

NORTH WESTERN · UNION PACIFIC · SOUTHERN PACIFIC

The Challenger
SAN FRANCISCO

NAME _____
ADDRESS _____
CITY _____ STATE _____

WORLD'S FAIR ST. LOUIS

MISSOURI PACIFIC RAILWAY

1904

ROUTE OF THE EAGLES

MISSOURI PACIFIC LINES

A SERVICE INSTITUTION

THE GEORGE WASHINGTON

Sleep like a Kitten

CHESAPEAKE and OHIO LINES

"El Capitan...
nothing like it in railroading"

◀ **advertising art,** 1950
A stylized painting depicts a Santa Fe
locomotive roaring through a remote
location on its way to a major city.

baggage label, 1948 ▶
The *El Capitan* logo was also worked
into a bold luggage label.

▲ advertisement (detail), 1942

This pastoral painting, created by the American Locomotive Company, shows locomotives with two types of power—diesel and steam—and suggests why both types of power were vital to the industry.

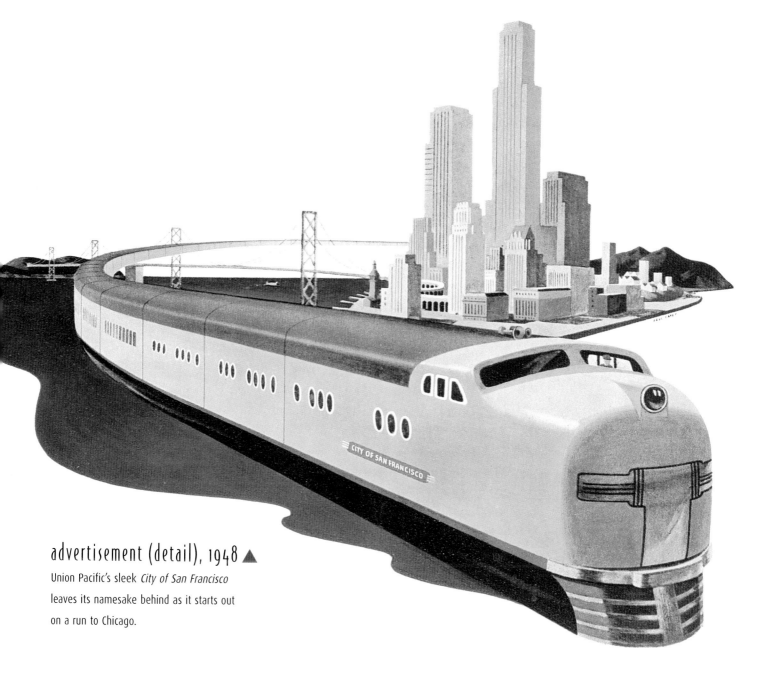

advertisement (detail), 1948 ▲

Union Pacific's sleek *City of San Francisco*
leaves its namesake behind as it starts out
on a run to Chicago.

ANOTHER NEW B&O FEATURE...

Private Rooms at LOW Coach Rates*

Slumbercoaches

on The Columbian

Strata-Dome Coach Dieseliner CHICAGO • WASHINGTON • BALTIMORE

* Regular Coach fare
plus a low space charge

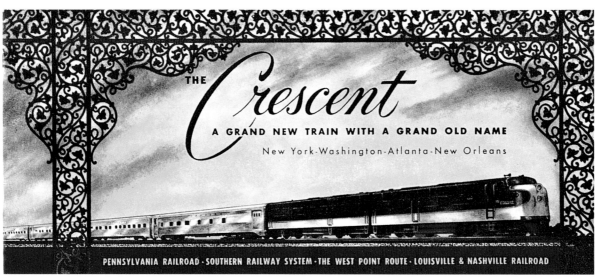

THE *Crescent*

A GRAND NEW TRAIN WITH A GRAND OLD NAME

New York-Washington-Atlanta-New Orleans

PENNSYLVANIA RAILROAD · SOUTHERN RAILWAY SYSTEM · THE WEST POINT ROUTE · LOUISVILLE & NASHVILLE RAILROAD

5 fine trains
daily to Chicago

**SUPER CHIEF
CHIEF
EL CAPITAN
GRAND CANYON
CALIFORNIA LTD.**

Visit GRAND CANYON • CARLSBAD CAVERNS • LAND OF PUEBLOS

Santa Fe

PAUL P. BRANCH, City Pass. Agent - M. J. PRATT, Pass. Agent - J. W. HARMAN, Pass. Agent - W. C. MUSICK, Pass. Agent - R. T. LAWRENCE, Pass. Agent - 222 So. Raymond Ave., Pasadena, Calif. - Phone SY 2-1191 - RY 1-6792

◀ **ticket holder, 1958**

As competition from the airlines increased, the rail companies were forced to lower fares as an inducement to keep passengers. This Baltimore & Ohio ticket holder is an example of such advertising.

◀ **ticket holder, 1940**

The *Crescent* was a deluxe streamliner service that ran between New York and New Orleans. Four companies combined forces to offer "a grand new train with a grand old name." New features included radios in every lounge, ice water, and five kinds of private rooms.

▲ **ink blotter, 1954**

Santa Fe's postwar West Coast to Chicago service was initially aimed at business travelers, but the concept of various vacation destinations was soon worked into the advertising.

◀ **advertisement, 1939**

Emphasizing its comfortable deluxe
Pullman service, the Pennsylvania
Railroad appealed to vacationers
to take the train.

photograph, 1948 ▶

This locomotive was an example of
Union Pacific's commitment to using
new designs for high horsepower
engines. Powered by gas turbine
engines, these locomotives moved
freight fast and effectively, and
earned the nickname "Verandas"
because of their long roofed walkways
that were used by crew members.

baggage label, 1938 ▶

Union Pacific's famous red, white, and blue shield logo yielded a striking luggage label. Union Pacific's rails followed the original "Overland Route" which was a natural thoroughfare for buffalo, fur traders, the Overland Stage, and the Pony Express.

MOBILE AND OHIO R.R.

DINING CARS

ALL TRAINS
ALL MEALS
A LA CARTE
ALL THE WAY
ALL THE TIME

THE **NATIONAL** LIMITED

Air-Conditioned Train between St. Louis, Cincinnati and Washington—Through Cars to and from New York.

NO EXTRA FARE

Baltimore & Ohio Railroad

LINKING 13 GREAT STATES
B&O
WITH THE NATION

RAIL FARES ARE CHEAP

ONE WAY IN COACHES
2¢ A MILE

B&O · B&O

ROUND TRIP IN COACHES
AS LOW AS
1½¢ A MILE

ANY DAY · ANYWHERE · BY TRAIN

FRISCO SYSTEM

CHICAGO AND **NorthWestern** SYSTEM

CHICAGO **MILWAUKEE** ST. PAUL AND PACIFIC

MAINE CENTRAL

CENTRAL OF GEORGIA RAILWAY CO.

See GLACIER PARK
PACIFIC NORTHWEST
ALASKA
Go **GREAT NORTHERN**

STREAMLINED DIESEL-POWERED

METEOR *ST. LOUIS—TULSA— OKLAHOMA CITY*

TEXAS SPECIAL *ST. LOUIS —TEXAS*

FRISCO

◀ baggage labels, 1936–1958

Various labels utilized to promote rail company logos and services.

▲ baggage label, 1956

Frisco Lines emphasized its streamlined diesels for the St. Louis to Texas run.

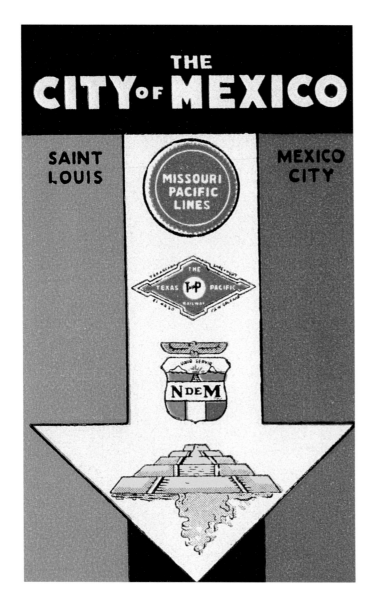

◀ **baggage label, 1938**

Missouri Pacific provided Saint Louis—
Mexico City service and produced this
very appropriate luggage label that
utilized Mexico's national colors.

baggage label, 1939 ▲

This bold North Western baggage
label proclaims that its *400* is "the
train that set the pace for the world."

baggage label, 1937 ▶

A die-cut Missouri Pacific baggage label both features the company's logo and emphasizes its air-conditioned trains—a luxury during the 1930s.

baggage label, 1950 ▶

This die-cut New York Central luggage label incorporates the company's strong logo as well as a locomotive.

the MERCURY
CHICAGO • DETROIT
TOLEDO • CLEVELAND
the MERCURY
E. FORSH

STREAMLINE

Art deco locomotives and their cars helped define a design movement

EVEN though the decade beginning in the late 1920s saw the industrialized world gripped by the Great Depression, the era also yielded some of the most distinctive design styles of the twentieth century. Known at the time as "streamline" or "moderne," in later years it was called "art deco," a term coined from the *Exposition Internationale des Arts Decoratifs et Industrials Modernes*, held in Paris in 1925, that revolutionized the design world.

The art deco period was filled with tapered, elegant shapes that ranged from stylish toasters to the towering stylized skyscrapers that thrust their pointed towers ever higher into the skies above American cities. With the proliferation of geometric products sweeping across the country, it was only natural that the world of the railways would be deeply and permanently changed. In fact, one of the terrains that best lent itself to the designers' lust for streamlined, clean, and efficient shapes was the new generation of massive locomotives and railroad cars.

Given the importance of the locomotive during this period, it is not surprising that many major designers would be attracted to creating their own stylized trains—machines that would embody the concept of streamlining with their sleek looks and suggestion of unlimited power, speed, and comfort. In a 1937 essay ("Locomotive," Raymond Loewy, Studio Publications), famed industrial designer Raymond Loewy commented, "My youth was charmed by the glamour of the locomotive. I am still under its spell. Unable to control an irresistible craving to sketch and dream locomotives at the oddest moments, it was a constant source of trouble during my college days, and the despair of my professors. Later, as a young man, it led to my complete oblivion as a dancing partner, for I spent long, enchanting hours at the locomotive depot instead of taking scheduled dance lessons. I have no regrets. In recent years it has been my privilege to design all sorts of things, such as streamlined ships, transcontinental motor buses, automobiles, and electric engines. Never did I dream that my career as an artist-engineer would lead me some day to that glorious adventure, the designing of a steam engine. And still the day has arrived. Last year, on March third, my first streamlined locomotive, developed in collaboration with the engineering department of the Pennsylvania Railroad, was placed in operation. It was an even greater thrill than I had expected. To Engine 3768, my heartiest wishes for a fast and brilliant career."

As America turned from an agrarian economy to one much more dependent upon industry, efficient rail, road, and air systems were rapidly put into effect. The influence of stream-lining was prevalent in this new industry, from the unmistakable impact of art deco upon the Douglas DC-3 airliner to locomotives featuring beautifully finished shells that were butt-welded for near-perfect smoothness and to eliminate "archaic" rivets. Even the powerful headlights were faired in for maximum sleekness. Stylized paint schemes and the wide use of stainless steel and polished aluminum also accented the streamlined conceit.

Graphic artists rapidly turned their attentions to promoting the streamline concept in transportation, and everything from baggage labels to magazine advertisements to posters to train schedules soon depicted cities as sprawling "Gothams," with skyscrapers piercing the heights and with all forms of transportation roaring in and out of the city, to promote an image of speed, prosperity, and futurism.

The railroads aggressively displayed their new streamliners at large public events, especially the 1939–1940 World's Fair in New York. Twenty-seven railroads joined together to cre-ate the Railroad Building, the largest freestanding structure at the event. Millions of visitors toured the building to view displays and such unusual performances as *Railroads on Parade,* a musical by

brochure, 1937

This stylized silver and blue brochure for the *City of Los Angeles* utilizes all the design conceits of art deco.

Kurt Weill that celebrated the meeting of the rails in 1869 at Promontory Point, Utah. The production was complete with cavalry and Indians, and the spectacle-hungry visitors enjoyed the show.

The star of the building's displays, however, was Raymond Loewy's one-million-pound steam locomotive, which had been built by the Pennsylvania Railroad. The 140-foot-long streamlined monster was kept fired up and running on a roller bed at a continuous speed of sixty-five miles per hour. To Americans just beginning to emerge from the grayness of the Depression, this streamliner signaled that a bright new future had arrived.

The railroads went out of their way to emphasize the term *streamliner* in their advertising, and the streamline concept was sometimes carried to extremes in the design of train-related ephemera, such as the martini glass on a Union Pacific cocktail coaster (surely a play on the popular *Thin Man* film series of the time period, in which stars Myrna Loy and William Powell consumed an impossible number of martinis and established that concoction as "the" drink of the streamline era) or the lovely winged design on an ink blotter given out to passengers aboard the *City of Los Angeles.*

Magazine advertising heralded "named" trains, such as the *20th Century Limited,* the *Mercury*, and the *Zephyr*—all names that connoted speed, comfort, and modernism. Advertising also pointed out such creature comforts as air conditioning (at a time when virtually no American household was similarly equipped), gourmet dining and bar service, and increased touring visibility through the new glass observation lounges that were being added to many passenger cars.

The streamline conceit lasted longer with the railroads than with any other form of American transportation, and streamline-type trains would survive into the 1960s; but the great art form that supported these exotic vehicles had really enjoyed its peak of creativeness during the 1930s and 1940s.

photograph, 1936 ▶

Raymond Loewy poses on the front of his first streamlined locomotive—Engine 3768—developed for the Pennsylvania Railroad and put into service in 1936. The stylized covering conceals a classic engine just like the locomotive pictured behind it.

▲ advertisements, 1938

The most famous of the streamliners was perhaps the *20th Century Limited,* and this advertising art depicts the glamor and excitement of traveling on this premium train.

▼ advertisement (detail), 1939

The drama, speed, and excitement of the *20th Century Limited* is effectively expressed in this thrusting image. Speeding between Chicago and New York (961 rail miles), the *20th Century*'s staff took deluxe care of its passengers; the train carried 2,500 pieces of linen and 2,500 pieces of china, silver, and stemware.

menu cover, 1939 ▶

An art deco menu for service aboard the *20th Century Limited*. The train was frequently ridden by Hollywood stars during the 1930s, and one waiter recalled that Spencer Tracy would wake at 5 a.m., order a full pot of black coffee, and then go back to sleep.

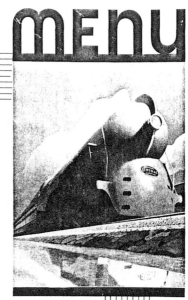

The 20th Century Limited
KNOWN THE WORLD OVER FOR
LUXURY AND DEPENDABILITY
New York . . . . Chicago

NEW YORK CENTRAL SYSTEM MORE THAN EVER—
IT PAYS TO RIDE THE CENTUR

◀◀ advertisement
(detail), 1949

The unveiling of a wildly futuristic *Hiawatha* streamliner at the Chicago Railroad Fair.

◀ advertisement
(detail), 1949

A picnicking couple watches the *Hiawatha* streamliner of the Milwaukee Road speed through a summer afternoon.

baggage labels, ▲
1928 (left) & 1940

Premium routes kept the same train name even though the trains would change as newer equipment became available, as seen by the locomotives depicted on different *Hiawatha* baggage labels.

timetable, 1954 ▶

The magic of the streamliner continued well into the 1950s, as illustrated by this Milwaukee Road schedule emphasizing its *Hiawatha* streamliners.

JUNE 20, 1954   JUNE 20, 1954

CHICAGO, MILWAUKEE, ST. PAUL AND PACIFIC RAILROAD

THE MILWAUKEE ROAD

THE MILWAUKEE ROAD

OLYMPIAN **Hiawatha** AND COLUMBIAN

CHICAGO · MILWAUKEE · ST. PAUL · MINNEAPOLIS
MILES CITY · BUTTE · SPOKANE · SEATTLE · TACOMA

TWIN CITIES   MIDWEST **Hiawathas**

CHICAGO · LA CROSSE · ST. PAUL · MINNEAPOLIS
DES MOINES · OMAHA · SIOUX CITY · SIOUX FALLS

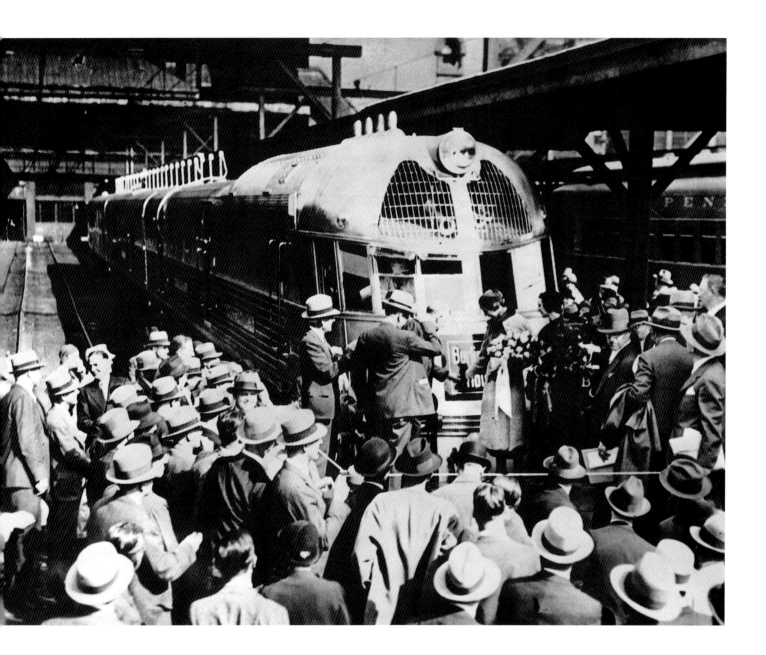

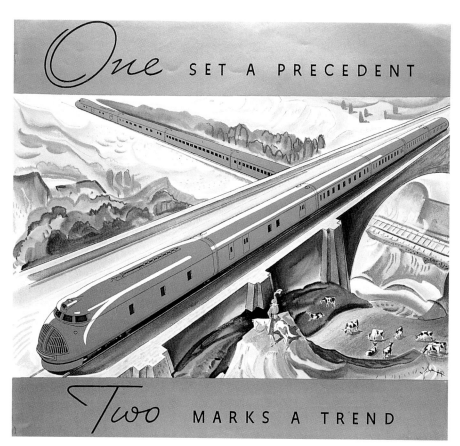

One SET A PRECEDENT

Two MARKS A TREND

▲ baggage label, 1935

Since many of the streamliners were made out of stainless steel or aluminum, baggage labels often reflected the sleek deco silver by utilizing silver foil. This example advertising the *Zephyr* emphasizes the fact that the train was "built of stainless steel."

◄ photograph, 1934

At the dedication ceremonies at Broad Street Station, Philadelphia, on April 18, 1934, Miss Marguerite Cotsworth christened Burlington's *Zephyr* No. 9900 with a bottle of champagne.

advertisement ▲
(detail), 1939

Alcoa Aluminum utilized this effective art to promote its all-aluminum streamliner operated by Union Pacific, which set a record time from New York to Los Angeles of 56 hours and 55 minutes.

◀ ticket holders, 1940

Aluminized paper created a bold art deco statement in these Santa Fe ticket holders.

baggage label, 1938 ▶

A bold and beautiful baggage label for Santa Fe's *Super Chief* streamliner.

brochure, 1938 ▼

The Pennsylvania Railroad used a streamliner image effectively on this brochure.

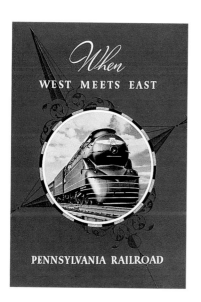

Streamliner

"CITY OF LOS ANGELES"

SWIFTLY, smoothly . . . past the twinkling lights
of towns . . . verdant valleys . . . rolling hills.
Train travel is stimulating, pleasurable. On the
"City of Los Angeles" it reaches a high peak of
enjoyment.

Daily . . . between Chicago and Los Angeles.

COACH OR PULLMAN

UNION PACIFIC RAILROAD

◄ advertisement, 1940

A stylish couple follows a laden porter
to the *City of Los Angeles*. Quite often,
streamliner service brought with it a
premium charge and advertising was
directed to appeal to society's upper
strata.

postcard, 1948 ▶

Union Pacific's *City of Los Angeles*
heads through a bleak, low desert
landscape.

▲ advertisement (detail), 1938

Night descends on a New York Central streamliner
accompanied by the copy, "One by one, the windows close
their eyes . . . for a wonderful Water Level Route sleep."
Companies gave considerable advertising space to promoting
the idea that the new streamliners were more comfortable and
offered better ride quality than the older trains.

baggage label, 1935 ▶

Baggage labels for Union Pacific–Southern Pacific–North Western streamliner service had a life preserver motif.

baggage label, 1940 ▼

This baggage label boldly promotes the fact that the streamliner *City of Denver* was the "world's fastest long distance train."

postcards, 1952 ▼

Streamliners were promoted in numerous ways, including this set of postcards which sold for 15 cents. The cards were published by Fred Harvey, the company that ran very popular restaurants at stations throughout the country.

**Domeliner
"CITY OF ST. LOUIS"**

UNION PACIFIC
Railroad

◀ baggage label, 1954

With the city looming in the background, a smart 1950s family prepares to board Union Pacific's *City of St. Louis* on this attractive baggage label.

 **photograph, 1958**

In a last-ditch attempt to attract passengers lured away by the airlines and the highways, the rather bulky *Aerotrain* attempted to blend a bit of futurism with streamlining. One prototype developed by General Motors is seen here on March 7, 1958 at San Diego Station during a nationwide tour. The concept did not meet with approval and General Motors dropped the project after investing millions of dollars.

brochure, 1938 ▶

This brochure art for Southern Pacific's new *Lark* streamliner takes full advertising advantage of the sleek train being admired by passengers.

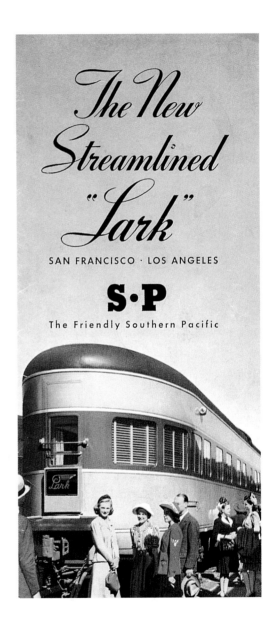

The New Streamlined "Lark"

SAN FRANCISCO · LOS ANGELES

S·P

The Friendly Southern Pacific

RAILS WEST

Rail travel not only helped to settle and populate the West, it also provided access to scenic vacation sites

THE battle to forge a transcontinental rail link remains one of America's great sagas. The endeavor involved pioneering exploration, incredible hardships, Indian wars, and the virtual slave labor of thousands of Chinese and Irish immigrants. The country was tied by rail from coast to coast at a waterless basin named Promontory Point, north of Utah's Great Salt Lake, on May 10, 1869. At 12:47 p.m., gold and silver spikes were hammered into the rails that had been slowly inching their way west and east. The coasts were now joined by an efficient transportation system that would allow rapid expansion and commerce without the hardships of that earlier form of heading west—the wagon train. Thus the image of the golden spike became part of American lore. However, reality was less than auspicious when Leland Stanford, imbibing champagne heavily in his deluxe coach car, took the silver-plated sledgehammer and completely missed his swing at the golden spike.

This unpropitious event capped an already tough push west, for anything west of the Mississippi River was considered by those on the East Coast as rather uncivilized. Early railroads often had no destinations, and many of the towns built around the rail lines were notorious places, such as Newton (known more commonly as "Shootin' Newton") and Dodge City, both in Kansas. These were lawless areas where everyone wore a six-shooter.

Rails soon branched into Texas, Wisconsin, Minnesota, and other territories that would become states. Rail companies undertook massive campaigns to attract settlers, even visiting foreign countries during the last two decades of the century to attract potential immigrants with tales—backed up with illustrated brochures and advertising—of cheap and lush farmland and idyllic homesteads. In reality, the farming in the American West was often brutal work in harsh weather conditions, but Germans and Scandinavians came by the thousands, often picking areas of the United States not dissimilar to their original homelands.

At the turn of the century, and as free time became more available to the expanding

baggage label, 1935

The national parks meant big business for railroads servicing those areas. Union Pacific offered transportation to the parks while promoting train travel comfort.

middle class, the idea of traveling to the western United States began to take hold as a result of heavy railroad advertising. These advertisements were Edwardian in concept, utilizing multiple ornate typefaces and detailed illustrations, depicting open coaches with well-dressed passengers leisurely chugging through painted deserts and over pastoral mountain ranges.

As the century progressed, so did the sophistication of advertising, and nearly every tool possible was utilized to promote the idea of train travel to the West, with its lure of open spaces and nearly year-round sunshine. The new national parks also proved to be a powerful draw, as thousands of visitors took the train to see these natural wonders which were often inaccessible except by rail. The concept of the West and the freedom the area offered was a strong pull for residents of the increasingly tightly packed East Coast. As can be seen on the following pages, railroad advertising took full advantage of the drama and native charm of what at the time was America's last frontier.

"*Whe-e-e-ew the New Super Chief!*"

advertisement ▶
(detail), 1946
Two young cowpokes are impressed
by the speed of the new *Super Chief.*

fast luxurious service to
California
LOS ANGELES · SAN DIEGO · SANTA BARBARA
Commencing December 28th, 1924

Golden State Limited

A completely new, de luxe, all-Pullman train. Most modern
sleeping, observation, club and through dining cars; lounging
room for ladies, maid and manicure, two baths, barber, valet.
TWO OTHER FAST DAILY TRAINS—Coaches, tourist and standard
sleepers, and dining cars. All trains leave Eastern terminals from Rock Island
stations, and Western terminals from Southern Pacific stations— via GOLDEN
STATE ROUTE—the short, interesting, mild-weather, low-altitude route.

For complete information, address office nearest to you

Southern Pacific
LINES
New York, 165 Broadway   Chicago, Southern Pacific Bldg.   Tucson, Score Bldg.
El Paso, 206 North Oregon St.   Los Angeles, Pacific Electric Bldg.

Commodious lounge
room, dressing room,
bath, manicure and
maid

Club car, shower, bar-
ber, and valet. Tele-
phones in terminals

Through dining cars,
always ready to serve
you meals of appetiz-
ing variety

Golden State Route
from CHICAGO ST. LOUIS MINNEAPOLIS ST. PAUL KANSAS CITY

Mardi Gras
at
New Orleans

See it on your Way to
California

ALL the gorgeous revelry of France and old
Madrid, joyous, carefree and colorful—a tale
from the Arabian Nights which comes to life each
year in America's most fascinating city.

See it without fail this year from February 11th
to 16th, on your way to California via the

SUNSET LIMITED

A splendid, de luxe daily train New Orleans to Los Angeles, San
Diego, and San Francisco. Stopovers at New Orleans allowed on
all tickets via Sunset Route.

Club Car, Observation Car and latest type Dining and Sleeping
Cars. Convenient service for the 120-mile motor side trip over the
famous Apache Trail and for the marvelous Carrizo Gorge.

*For further information and descriptive booklets
address any of the following offices:*

New York   Chicago   New Orleans
165 Broadway   15 W. Jackson Blvd.   Pan Am. Bank Bldg.
Los Angeles   Houston   San Francisco
Pacific Electric Bldg.   Southern Pacific Bldg.   Southern Pacific Bldg.

Sunset Route

SOUTHERN PACIFIC LINES

▲ advertisement, 1925

This idealized scene of well-dressed
passengers waving at an Indian chief
who just happens to be standing by
the rails was typical of the period.

advertisement, 1926 ▲

Advertisements for the Sunset Route
of Southern Pacific were designed to
lure passengers to California with the
interesting diversions on the way.

photograph, 1910 ▶

Four ladies pose for a portrait on
the promenade deck of Santa Fe's
California Limited prior to a trip
west.

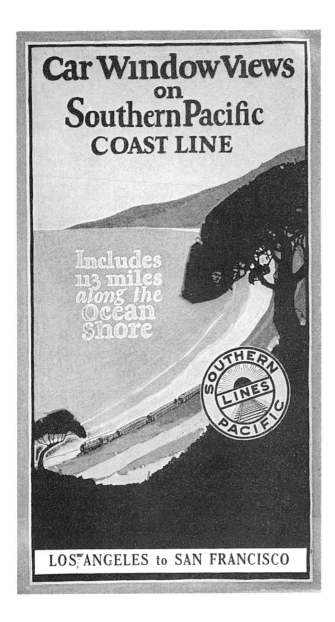

◀ **timetable, 1924**

This craftsman-style illustration highlights the 113 miles of oceanside rail tracks on Southern Pacific's Los Angeles-to-San Francisco service.

baggage labels, 1930-40 ▶

Some of the most collectable items associated with railway advertising are baggage labels, and these examples show some of the diversity in style. Wonderful "Buffalo Bill" art (1930) graces a die-cut baggage label advertising the Burlington Route's Cody Road to Yellowstone Park. An appropriate wagon train motif is used on the 1940 label for the combined North Western, Union Pacific, and Southern Pacific *Forty Niner* service. A powerful image for the *Californian* on this 1936 label also promoted the connecting service with the Southern Pacific and Rock Island Line. The populist statement "go home by train" is surrounded by the logos of three railroads on this 1940 label.

YELLOWSTONE PARK
VIA
CODY ROAD

Burlington
Route

NAME
ADDRESS
CITY   STATE

THE FORTY NINER

NORTH WESTERN · UNION PACIFIC · SOUTHERN PACIFIC

The Californian

NAME

SOUTHERN PACIFIC ★ ROCK ISLAND

WESTERN PACIFIC
FEATHER RIVER ROUTE

Santa Fe

SOUTHERN PACIFIC
LINES

PROPERTY OF

NAME

ADDRESS

CITY

GO HOME BY TRAIN

◀ label, 1939

This Railway Express label symbolically presents various forms of transport to the West. It also highlights the New York World's Fair and San Francisco's Golden Gate International Exposition.

poster, 1935 ▶

As a remote train rumbles through a mountain pass, a ghostly rider acknowledges the new form of transport that would soon pose a threat to passenger railways—a Boeing 247 airliner.

RAILWAY EXPRESS

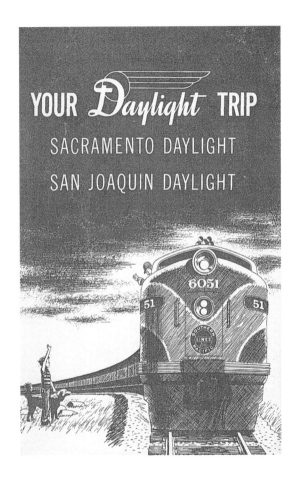

 **timetable, 1951**

A boy and his dog accentuate the rural theme of the Southern Pacific Railroad's service through California's Central Valley.

advertisement, 1937 ▲

This full-page ad from the *Saturday Evening Post* highlighted Southern Pacific's *Daylight* streamliner service.

Southern Pacific *Daylight*

LOS ANGELES - SAN FRANCISCO

Daylight

NAME

ADDRESS

CITY   STATE

◀ **baggage label, 1935**

Southern Pacific's *Daylight* stream-liner label carries distinctive bold graphics along with a stylized winged emblem.

▼ **sticker, 1950**

The Southern Pacific streamliner *Daylight* roars past a California mission setting on this sticker advertising its Los Angeles–San Francisco run.

LOS ANGELES · SAN FRANCISCO

THE NEW *Daylight*

SOUTHERN PACIFIC

brochure, 1932 ▶

National parks provided a bread-and-butter business for the railroads servicing those areas, and company artists went out of their way to create appealing images. An example is this Union Pacific brochure for "all expense escorted tours" of Yellowstone, Zion–Bryce, and Grand Canyon National Parks.

◀ brochure, 1930

Union Pacific advertised the
Boulder Dam Route so that
vacationers could view one of
the "wonders of the world."

along
your
way

Facts about stations and
scenes on the Santa Fe

Santa Fe

▲ brochure, 1940

This promotional brochure cover
illustrates Santa Fe trains delivering
passengers in an extremely idealized
western setting.

▼ **advertisement, 1954**

An idealized western evening landscape entices easterners in this
Santa Fe winter-vacation promotion.

**advertisement ▲
(detail), 1948**

Whenever possible, Santa Fe advertisements used the "Chief" image. In this
instance, an appropriately attired young
lad receives a friendly wave from the
engineer aboard the *Super Chief.*

◀ advertisement
(detail), 1961

Free-form water color illustration promotes "fresh as a breeze" traveling and highlights the comforts of Union Pacific's Pullman service.

baggage labels, ▶
1925 (top), 1948
photograph, n.d.

Although numerous historic train stations across the United States have been destroyed in the quest for "progress," Los Angeles' magnificent Union Station remains a proud and well-maintained city landmark. Not only does it still function as a main terminal destination, it also appears in many Hollywood film and television productions.

LOS ANGELES CALIF.

NEW UNION STATION

MAIN ENTRANCE UNION STATION
LOS ANGELES · CALIFORNIA

A CERTAIN ELEGANCE

Railway posters in Britain and Europe often reflected fine art

IN many ways, Britain and the United States paralleled each other in the development of efficient trains—although the British Isles certainly could not match the vast distances of the United States. During the 1800s, there was a great deal of public skepticism about trains and they were often viewed as extremely dangerous affairs. The British public was shocked in 1842 when Queen Victoria made a train trip from Slough to London. Although the engine was under the command of famed mechanical engineer Isambard Kingdom

Brunel, the public thought train travel much too dangerous for the Queen, who apparently thoroughly enjoyed her adventure. There were reasons for the public's apprehension; British trains were not required to have seats until 1844, and that took an act of Parliament. Prior to that time, passengers were simply herded aboard cars and left to their own devices. Before the turn of the century, rail advertising did exist in Britain, but it was usually in the form of crowded letterpress ads that were mainly type and extremely cluttered. With the new century, however, rapid developments in color lithography allowed a completely new kind of advertisement to be created. Unfortunately, there was a great deal of holdover from earlier efforts, and these new posters were equally cluttered and difficult to read, although they did now offer color. These early color advertisements usually promoted resorts that could be easily reached by rail, and the main goal of the designers seemed to be to crowd as much on one page as possible.

As time went on, several of the large rail companies started their own art and advertising departments and quality gained sophistication in an effort to capture the public's imagination. These inexpensively produced posters were one of the few ways the general public could be made aware of a particular product or service since media services lagged behind the U.S. in variety. The walls of London buildings as well as the expanding Underground "tube" system were often plastered with a bewildering array of posters calling for the viewer's attention.

As graphic quality began to increase, rail companies developed their own advertising "style" that could easily be identified by the traveling public. The onset of the Great War put a rapid end to such endeavors, however, as Britain prepared to endure four years of conflict.

With the end of the war, the railroads restarted their artistic appeals to the public. Posters became extremely popular in the Underground system, where they once again had to com-

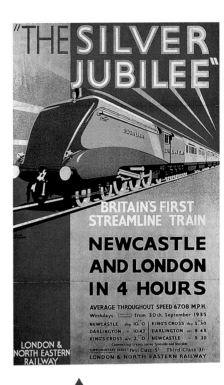

▲

poster, 1935

As in the United States, British artists responded enthusiastically to the introduction of the new streamliners and began including the locomotives to a greater degree in their art. Utilizing cool colors, Frank Newbould's poster proclaims the striking image of the Silver Jubilee as being "Britain's first streamline train."

pete with a myriad of other ads. It became apparent that rail art could not be effective if it was hard to see and read. Accordingly, certain areas of the Underground system were set aside for rail publicity alone, so that it did not get lost in the numbers of ads flooding the "tube." With better visibility, artists had greater motivation to improve their work, and the Underground soon became both a patron of artists and an important place for their work to be seen.

New type styles were created that came to be associated with Underground rail art, and the overall result was the creation of some very impressive advertising art that was "user friendly" for the increasingly large traveling public. This new rail art was even deemed by one critic as a "reform movement in advertising." Many of the posters created to promote travel to Britain's scenic or commercial locales did not feature anything remotely associated with the rails, usually relying on historic or important features of areas being visited. When shown, trains were often relegated to small images in an idealized landscape. Today, these posters are extremely collectable and have shown constant appreciation in value.

On the Continent, rail art took a different form. Beginning the century nearly as cluttered as its British counterpart, Continental rail art soon began finding its own style and rapidly came to rely on the new modernism to promote travel. Also, the Europeans were much less cautious about including the train in their art. With the advent of art deco, French artists created some of the most spectacular rail images ever seen.

When George Mortimer Pullman revolutionized train travel in the United States with the introduction of his Pullman luxury cars in 1864, the Pullman Palace Car Company soon attracted the attention of the Europeans. In France, Georges Nagelmackers became an instant fan of the Pullman car and began building his own luxury sleeping cars. In 1872, he formed the Compagnie Internationale des Wagons-Lits, soon combining with

poster, 1929

W. S. Bylitiphs' painting for Wagons-Lits advertised the company's new *Golden Arrow* service from London to Paris. Note the prominent Pullman logo on the side of the car.

▼

Colonel William Mann to start a regular deluxe sleeping-car line. Wagons-Lits greatly expanded its service and attempted to penetrate the British market, but with little success. In 1883, the Express d'Orient line went into operation between Paris and Constantinople, and in 1888 it was extended to London utilizing British operators on that side of the Channel. In 1891, the Express d'Orient was officially renamed the Orient Express, and the world's most recognized rail name was created.

Over the years, a fabulous amount of advertising art was created to bring attention to this very famous service. Closed for the two World Wars (during which time a great deal of its rolling stock was destroyed in combat), the line once again started operations in 1946. By the 1970s, the Orient Express was distinctly shabby and on its way downhill; on May 19, 1977, the last direct run was completed, and many of the cars were placed for auction. Fortunately, these cars, with their rare wood inlays and Lalique glass panels, were often purchased by collectors. James B. Sherwood, president of the Sea Containers Group, began to buy these cars with the idea of restoring them and recreating the Orient Express in all its prewar drama and elegance.

This he did, and on May 25, 1982, after great expense, Sherwood launched the inaugural run of the Venice Simplon-Orient-Express from Victoria Station in London to Venice. Since then, the deluxe route has expanded and become extremely popular with well-heeled travelers, and the new company has generated its own collection of advertising art to continue the glamor of this famous line.

photograph, n.d. ▶

Passengers stretch their legs while the Orient Express pauses on its way through Bulgaria. The train left Istanbul every evening at nine and passed through Bulgaria, Yugoslavia, Italy, and Switzerland before arriving in Paris three days later.

◀ **map, 1930**

An attractive art deco route map illustrated the combined routes of the Simplon-Orient-Express and the Taurus Express.

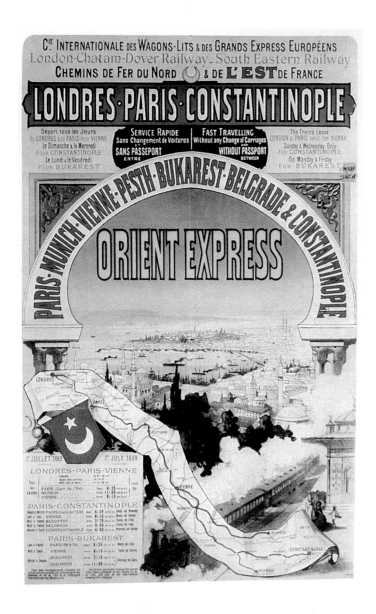

◀ poster, 1889

Packed with type and illustrations, this Orient Express poster showed the sights (as well as a map) for the train's adventurous route between London and Constantinople with main stops in Paris, Munich, Vienna, Belgrade, and Budapest.

poster, 1906 ▶

A Simplon-Express poster by artist Henry Mouren highlighted the attractive locales serviced by the train after the opening of the Simplon Tunnel. A great engineering feat begun in 1898 and completed in 1906, this 12-mile tunnel through the Alps connected the Paris-to-Venice run to the Brussels–Vienna route.

poster, 1924 ▶▶

The Simplon-Express became the Simplon-Orient-Express in 1919 when the route was once again extended to Constantinople (now known as Istanbul). The Taurus-Express continued the route as far as Cairo.

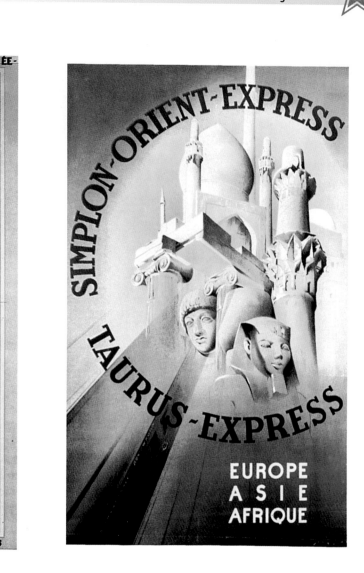

poster, 1927 ▶

A striking A. M. Cassandre poster
for *Étoile du Nord* service with
emphasis on the Pullman cars.

◀ poster, 1928

Travel from Calais to the Côte d'Azur on Wagons-Lits' *Train Bleu* was effectively portrayed in this poster by Zenobel.

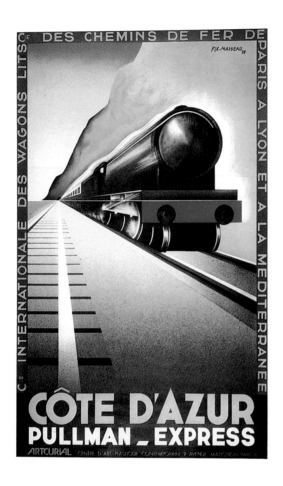

◀ **poster, 1929**

Pierre Fix-Masseau's poster for Wagons-Lits advertising its Côte d'Azur Pullman Express service. Fix-Masseau was hired by the restructured Venice Simplon-Orient-Express during the 1980s to create a new series of posters.

poster, 1932 ▼

Pierre Fix-Masseau's very collectable *Exactitude* poster for the French line Etat.

poster, 1927

This magnificent art deco poster by Cassandre brings high prices at auction. The work was originally published (and has been reproduced many times) for a combined-service route that included Chemin de fer du nord in conjunction with Southern Railway, Chemins de fer Belges, Deutsche Reichsbahn Ges., Polskie koleje panstwowe, and Compagnie des Wagons-Lits. Utilizing new Pullman cars, the route was a first-class service. This was one of the first European posters to put emphasis on the train itself—trains had been considered rather unattractive, hence the usual reliance on painting some interesting point of the train's destination. Cassandre would later state, "A painting is an end in itself. The poster is only a means to an end, a means of communication between the dealer and the public, something like a telegraph."

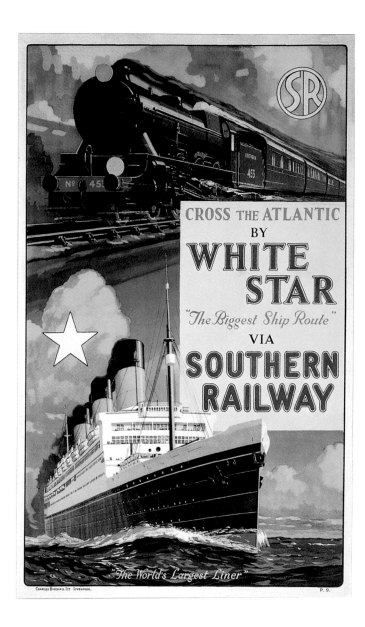

◀ poster, 1926

A Southern Railway poster that ties in transatlantic travel with White Star liners. Painted by William McDowell, this is a very collectable poster.

poster, 1931 ▶

The purchase of Pullman-style cars gave British train travelers a new era of luxury; the *Bournemouth Belle* was an all-Pullman extra-charge service.

poster, 1937 ▶▶

Bryan de Grineau made dramatic use of the *Coronation Scot,* which was the first streamliner to run between England and Scotland, often hitting speeds over 100 miles per hour.

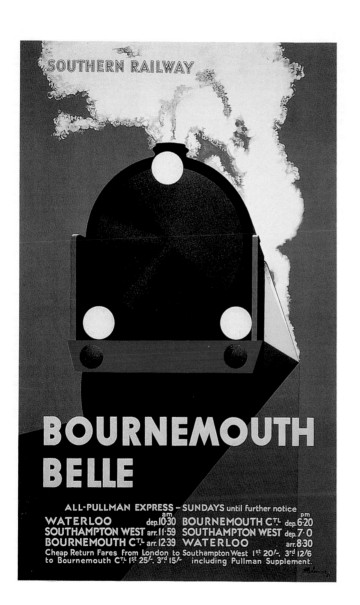

SOUTHERN RAILWAY

BOURNEMOUTH BELLE

ALL-PULLMAN EXPRESS – SUNDAYS until further notice

	am		pm
WATERLOO	dep.10·30	BOURNEMOUTH C^{TL.}	dep.6·20
SOUTHAMPTON WEST	arr.11·59	SOUTHAMPTON WEST	dep.7·0
BOURNEMOUTH C^{TL.}	arr.12·39	WATERLOO	arr.8·30

Cheap Return Fares from London to Southampton West 1st 20/- 3rd 12/6
to Bournemouth C^{TL.} 1st 25/- 3rd 15/- including Pullman Supplement.

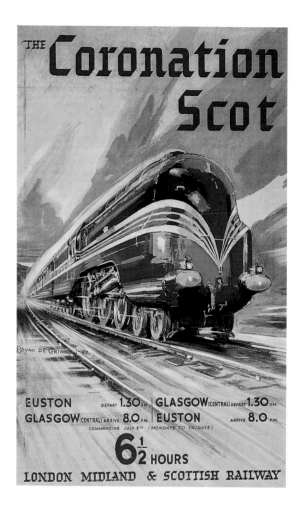

THE Coronation Scot

EUSTON DEPART 1.30 A.M. | GLASGOW (CENTRAL) DEPART 1.30 P.M.
GLASGOW (CENTRAL) ARRIVE 8.0 P.M. | EUSTON ARRIVE 8.0 P.M.
COMMENCING JULY 5TH (MONDAYS TO FRIDAYS)

6½ HOURS

LONDON MIDLAND & SCOTTISH RAILWAY

◀ **poster, 1929**

Not surprisingly, many staid British considered this poster offensive. The bold use of design and color was in opposition to the pastoral travel poster favored by the majority of the British public. A publication of the time commented, "the poster is of curious design, but very effective, the colouring being of a vivid order, and the letterpress consisting of the company's monogram and the words 'South for Winter Sunshine.'" Painted by Edmond Vaughan for Southern Railway.

poster, 1936 ▶

A. R. Thomson makes good use of
the sleek shape of *The Flying
Scotsman* for this London & North
Eastern Railway poster. Note the
statement at bottom right: "with
apologies to the Southern Railway."
In 1932, Southern Railway's art
department created an extremely
popular poster of a young lad talking
to the train engineer. The poster itself
was inspired by a 1924 photograph
taken by famed transportation photog-
rapher Charles Brown at the end of
one of the Waterloo Station platforms.
Initially issued in a run of just 3,000
posters, the image was so appealing
to the British public that it went back
to press many times. The popularity
of the poster started a search for the
young boy, who was eventually found
living in California with his parents
after emigrating from Britain. Oddly,
the much more sophisticated LNER
poster was not a hit and was not
reprinted after its initial run.

IM TAKING AN
EARLY HOLIDAY COS
I KNOW SUMMER
COMES SOONEST IN THE SOUTH
SOUTHERN RAILWAY

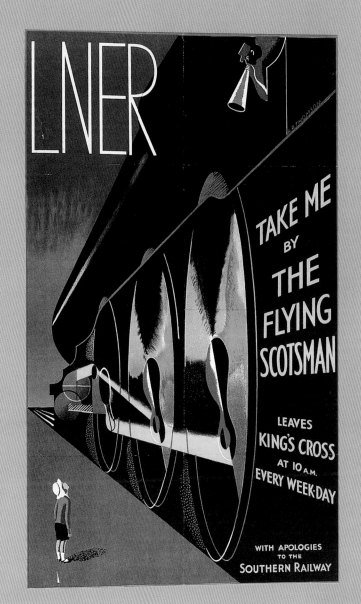

LNER

TAKE ME
BY
THE
FLYING
SCOTSMAN

LEAVES
KING'S CROSS
AT 10 A.M.
EVERY WEEK-DAY

WITH APOLOGIES
TO THE
SOUTHERN RAILWAY

poster, 1937 ▶

Another example of poster art that does not feature trains is this rather ominous view of the Tower of London, executed for the Great Western Railway by Frank Mason.

poster, 1938 ▶▶

A striking Great Western Railway poster *Speed to the West* illustrates all the power of a steam locomotive trailing a dappled layer of smoke. This fine piece of art is the work of Charles Mayo.

THE RIVER CAMEL NEAR PADSTOW

SEE THE WEST COUNTRY FROM THE TRAIN
BY
SOUTHERN RAILWAY

◀ **poster, 1947**

As in many other British rail posters, the train forms only a small part of the overall art in this detail of Eric Hesketh Hubbard's painting *The River Camel Near Padstow* for the Southern Railway.

poster (detail), 1935 ▶

A lovely pastoral detail from a London Midland & Scottish Railway poster illustrating the Britannia Tubular Bridge in Wales. Executed by Norman Wilkinson.

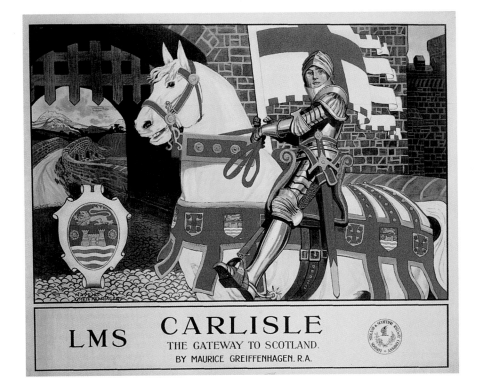

LMS **CARLISLE**
THE GATEWAY TO SCOTLAND.
BY MAURICE GREIFFENHAGEN. R.A.

◀ poster, 1924

British rail posters, often the most common means of advertising rail travel in that country, frequently had little or nothing to do with rail equipment. Posters such as *Carlisle— The Gateway to Scotland* were available for purchase by the general public and were very popular. This London Midland and Scottish poster by Maurice Greiffenhagen, part of the Royal Academy Series, emphasized the history of the area rather than rail transportation.

poster, 1946 ▶

This postwar painting by Terence Cuneo titled *The Day Begins* shows a London Midland and Scottish Railway locomotive being made ready for a day's work.

 THE DAY BEGINS

HEADING NORTH

Modernized railways opened vast areas of the United States and Canada to business and tourism

RAIL schedules were among the first scheduled routines thrust upon the American public—a mainly rural public more accustomed to seasons than to daily or weekly timetables. With the advent of popularized rail travel in the nineteenth century, however, schedules became a constant fact of American life. As a nation, we began to look less to the sun, moon, and weather and more at the printed page that announced arrivals and departures. Trains bearing passengers, freight, and vital equipment for an increasingly industrialized twentieth century linked many facets of life to the schedules of locomotives pounding down glistening lines of steel rails.

photograph, 1934

Commodore Vanderbilt entered service in 1934 to haul the New York Central System's premier *20th Century Limited* train. Detailed in the best art deco design, the locomotive was finished in a gloss gun-metal gray lacquer with fine silver striping. The elegant shape hid the fact that underneath was a regular Hudson-type steam locomotive. However, the decorative wrapping did have advantages as wind tunnel tests showed that the shape cut drag by 35 percent.

The inception of regularly scheduled rail service helped develop the Northwestern United States as well as the huge landmass of Canada. Before regular airline service, one could only get across Canada via rail, unless the traveler would brave a series of flights undertaken by the primitive bush planes that began plying remote Canadian skies during the mid-1920s.

Train travelers were lured in increasing numbers soon after the turn of the century into visiting the virtually unspoiled beauty of the American Northwest, and many advertisements touted the numerous national parks. Great Northern produced a variety of advertising materials illustrating the wonders of the Northwest, with emphasis placed on the suggestion to "See America First." Some of the images, such as the label for Glacier Park, included views of both scenic parks and Native Americans in traditional clothing.

In Canada, some of the world's best rail advertising art was created by Canadian Pacific. Formed in 1881, with the mandate of building a rail line from eastern Canada to the Pacific Ocean, the company set out to create an absolutely first-class operation; the last spike on this wildly ambitious project was driven in 1885, nearly five years ahead of the deadline that had been negotiated with the Canadian government.

A believer in poster art, the company produced an increasingly effective series of images for all their forms of travel—the artwork on a poster promoting winter sports in Quebec is as clean and sharp-edged as a winter day in that province, while the simple but visually bold 1925 poster promoting cross-country service on the pioneering Trans-Canada Limited appeals to the sense of adventure. While the trains opened these areas to the public, the advertising art also established new means of capturing the general public's increasing interest in travel for pleasure.

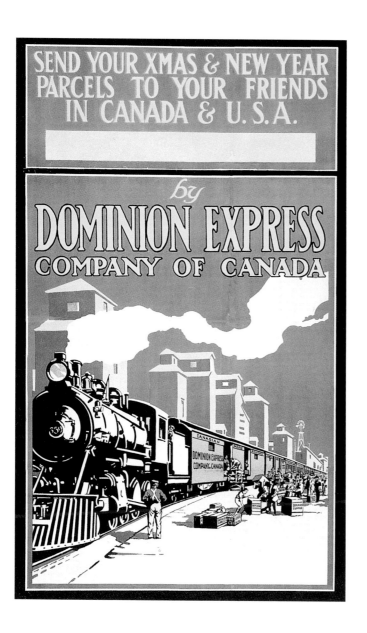

◄◄ poster, 1895

Not only did Canadian Pacific advertise to tourists visiting Canada in this
turn-of-the-century poster, but the
company also offered an amazing
array of other global services. This
poster was designed to be placed
in various travel locations around
Britain to entice the British traveler.

◄ poster, 1910

With grain elevators starkly rising
in the background, freight and mail
are loaded aboard a Canadian
Pacific train in conjunction with the
Dominion Express Company of
Canada. The two businesses combined forces to insure quick transportation of goods and supplies by
rail into remote farm areas.

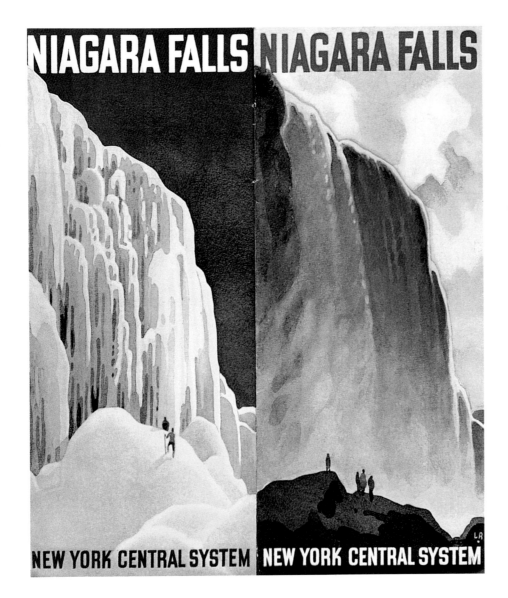

advertisement ▶ (detail), 1954

As with railways in the United States, Canada's railways introduced more modern equipment to counter the threat posed by airlines and automobiles.

◀ timetable, 1938

New York Central System's Niagara Falls timetable dramatically illustrates reasons for visiting the joint Canadian/American natural wonder during different seasons.

map, 1938 ▶

Canadian Pacific set up offices throughout North America and Europe to promote travel in Canada. This tourist map offered "the scenic route across Canada."

logo, 1950 ▶▶

This Great Northern Railway logo illustrates that the train could take vacationers directly to natural wonders.

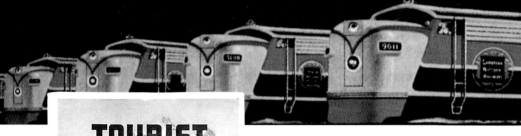

TOURIST
MAP
OF
CANADA

The
SCENIC ROUTE
ACROSS
CANADA

CANADIAN NATIONAL
To Everywhere in Canada

CANADIAN
NATIONAL
RAILWAYS

THE ONLY RAILWAY SERVING ALL 10
PROVINCES OF CANADA

GREAT NORTHERN
RAILWAY

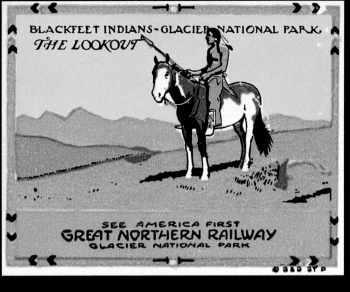

◁ labels, 1936

Great Northern produced a series of small labels and stamps promoting travel to national parks, often utilizing bold images of Native Americans.

timetable, 1939 ▷

A Great Northern schedule for Canada's Waterton Lakes Park superimposes the company's bold logo over a pastoral setting illustrating the lodge on the lake.

poster, 1937 ▶

Utilizing bold colors and primary graphics, this attractive Canadian Pacific poster presents a forceful enticement to vacation in Canada.

◀ **poster, 1930**

As skiing became a more popular pastime, Canadian Pacific let travelers know the rail line could supply service to some excellent ski areas. On this poster, two stylized skiers dominate the ice-skaters in the background.

poster, 1947 ▶

With the end of World War II, rail travel was once again opened up to the general public. The sight of a locomotive speeding from a tunnel, with towering mountains forming an imposing background, personified the hard-won freedom.

▼ poster, 1925

The Trans-Canada Limited offered deluxe amenities and an incredibly scenic ride across the country. This poster by Gordon Fraser Gillespie certainly portrays the grandeur of the journey.

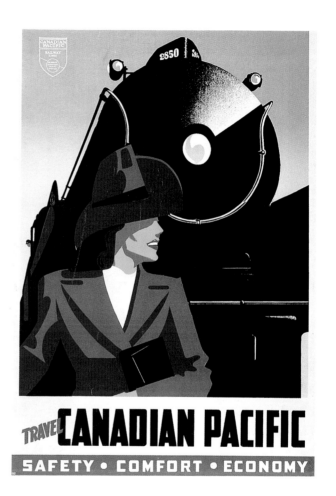

poster, 1940 ▲

The image of a modern woman with modern transportation is effectively presented in this Peter Ewart silk screen.

poster, 1955 ▶

Canadian Pacific's *Canadian* winds through the country's natural beauty in this Roger Couillard photolithograph.

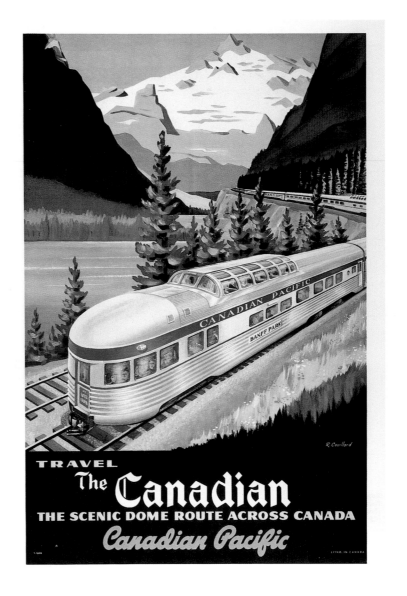

▼ label, 1937

This odd Northern Pacific label lists many of the locations visited by the company on "The Route of the Great Big Baked Potato."

advertisement, 1939 ▲

Advertisements encouraging travel to the North often made use of animals indigenous to the area, in this instance a moose.

Railroads were essential to America's World War 2 effort and the era produced some distinctive artwork

RAILS FOR

VICTORY

WITH the December 7, 1941, Japanese attack on Pearl Harbor, America found itself in a world war for which the nation was not really prepared. As Europe and the Far East became embroiled in separate conflicts in the late 1930s, a large portion of the American population favored isolationism. America's tremendous industrial might, however, was greatly appreciated by nations such as Britain and France, which realized that American factories could rapidly produce the armaments they needed so desperately even though the weapons, especially aircraft, were not up to the latest standards of European combat.

The European orders that greatly boosted America's industrial might also had beneficial effects on other aspects of industry, especially the railroad system. What the United States did have in place was a large and fairly efficient rail network, and nearly every large military plant had its own rail spur. This allowed rapid transportation of completed weapons or components to harbors, where they could be shipped to their eagerly waiting customers.

Fortunately, this system was up and functioning when President Franklin Roosevelt declared in December 1941 that the United States was at war with the Axis. Huge orders for military goods flooded America's factories, and virtually all production in the country became devoted to the war effort. Detroit quit making cars and turned its efficient methods of mass production into building tanks, aircraft, and engines. The rail system began to function on a nonstop basis as raw materials were brought into the factories and completed weapons shipped out. Also, since the railroads could operate without the direct threat of enemy attack (although considerable precautions were undertaken to prevent sabotage), a twenty-four-hour, seven-day-a-week system of nationwide transport was brought into command. Seats for civilians became a premium on passenger trains.

As American industry rapidly expanded with the war effort, the railroads mounted a large advertising campaign to illustrate that they were doing their part in the battle for final victory. One of the most popular victory slogans was "Keep 'Em Flying," which related to Roosevelt's promise to build 50,000 aircraft per year. The railroads quickly, and cleverly, modified the slogan to "Keep 'Em Rolling" to bring emphasis to the importance of keeping the railroads working at their peak during the conflict. (Throughout the war, railroads provided 97 percent of the transportation for military personnel traveling on duty, while also carrying over 90 percent of military freight.)

The advertising artwork during this period was propaganda at its best, utilizing patriotic themes and images executed in bold primary colors. Since there was some stigma attached to men not in military uniforms, some railroad ads and posters stressed that a man in railroad work clothes was a man in uniform; there was a great deal of truth in this since the government considered railroad-related employment as vital to the nation's defense.

To emphasize the fact that railroads and the military were working closely, and vitally, together, rail workers were often portrayed in their work clothes alongside men in uniform. Strong slogans like "Give 'em Hell, Pals" were backed up with equally strong patriotic artwork that brought the statement home forcefully. The image of a soldier of near-Goliath proportions in several ads emphasized that each fighting man had to be backed up by eight tons of supplies and equipment, most of which would be moved by rail. The war years were not a time of understated advertising.

Union Pacific produced a series of posters (which were also reproduced as large stamps that could be collected in a booklet or affixed to mail) that emphasized the importance of railroads to the war effort. Utilizing the "Keep 'Em Rolling" theme, the aggressive artwork was filled with patriotic statements.

When the United States entered the war, the thrust of railroad art and advertising completely changed. The Pennsylvania Railroad produced a highly collectable series of calendars and the paintings during the war years were executed by the well-known artists Grif Teller, Alexander Leydenfrost, and Dean Cornwell. For the 1943 calendar, Cornwell produced *Serving the Nation,* a work that leaves little to the imagination as freight trains speed to and from looming factories, with loads of coal going one direction and completed battle tanks heading the other way. The entire scene is dominated by Uncle Sam rolling up his sleeves and glaring out over the

map, 1944

In a time of heightened national security, this curious map gave Union Pacific passengers a look at the many military facilities located on their route.

distant horizon. The painting was so popular that it was reproduced in numerous magazines, including *Life.*

The huge success of *Serving the Nation* led the Pennsylvania Railroad to commission Cornwell again for the 1944 calendar. This time, the artist chose to paint in earthen tones, but he still used an allegorical sky to advantage. With factories in the background and a farmer on a tractor in the foreground, a freight locomotive thunders by on a wartime mission. The sky area is filled with an amazing depiction of American troops and Sherman tanks battling forward under enemy fire. Two American forty-eight-star flags draw attention to the flags of the marines, Coast Guard, army, and navy. Once again, the painting was a success and was widely reproduced in numerous formats.

Today, rail artwork from the war years is highly collectable, since it graphically portrays a brief period in history when the entire nation functioned as one unit directed toward a common goal.

"TOURISTS" in our western wonderland

advertisement (detail), 1944

A detail of an unusual piece of art from a Southern Pacific advertisement came with the statement that "Southern Pacific is host to thousands of men in uniform who are now visiting the West for the first time. Some had never been aboard a train till war came. Many had never been very far away from their home city or village. These bright, sturdy youngsters with faces pressed against our train windows, what do they think of our western country? Will they want to travel here again after the war when they can do what they please?"

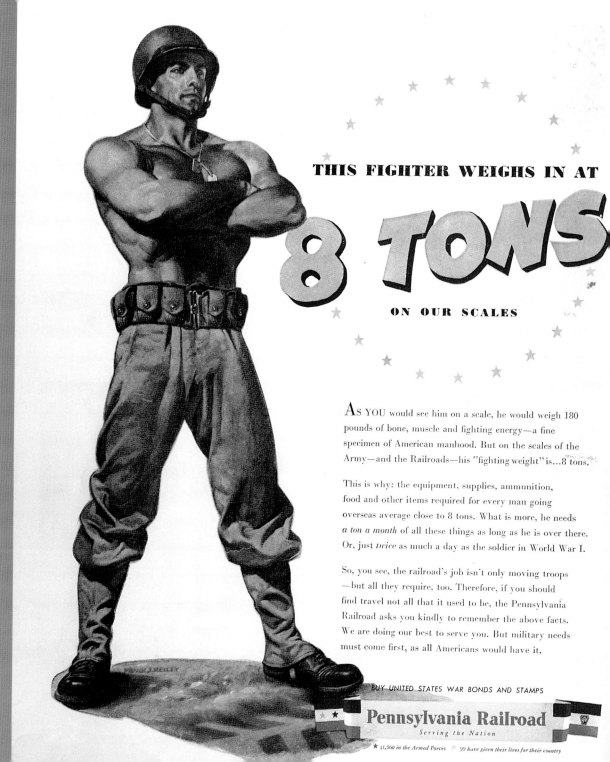

THIS FIGHTER WEIGHS IN AT

8 TONS

ON OUR SCALES

As you would see him on a scale, he would weigh 180 pounds of bone, muscle and fighting energy—a fine specimen of American manhood. But on the scales of the Army—and the Railroads—his "fighting weight" is...8 tons.

This is why: the equipment, supplies, ammunition, food and other items required for every man going overseas average close to 8 tons. What is more, he needs *a ton a month* of all these things as long as he is over there. Or, just *twice* as much a day as the soldier in World War I.

So, you see, the railroad's job isn't only moving troops —but all they require, too. Therefore, if you should find travel not all that it used to be, the Pennsylvania Railroad asks you kindly to remember the above facts. We are doing our best to serve you. But military needs must come first, as all Americans would have it.

BUY UNITED STATES WAR BONDS AND STAMPS

Pennsylvania Railroad
Serving the Nation

★ 41,560 in the Armed Forces ★ 99 have given their lives for their country

▲ **calendar art, 1943**

Serving the Nation, Dean Cornwell's stunning art for the Pennsylvania Railroad's 1943 calendar, is an allegorical portrayal of trains hauling raw materials and returning with combat-ready equipment.

▲ calendar art, 1944

Dean Cornwell's painting *Forward* for
the Pennsylvania Railroad.

◀ poster/stamp, 1945

During World War II, Union Pacific produced a series of images that were printed both as large stamps and as posters. Usually propagandistic in nature, the stamps could be affixed to letters to promote patriotism on the home front, while the posters often decorated Union Pacific terminals to emphasize the line's work in the war effort.

poster/stamp, 1944 ▶

This attractive airbrush-enhanced poster shows the railroad's important role in bringing combat materials to shipping points for transfer to the world's battlefronts.

▼ advertisement
(detail), 1943

This symbolic painting from Rock
Island Lines is accompanied by copy
that states, "Rock Island Lines,
against a backdrop of proud glorious
yesterdays, pledges that it shall take
a hand in providing the bright future
you are hoping for."

advertisement ▲
(detail), 1943

The Milwaukee Road's streamliner
heads in one direction with troops
aboard, while freight cars roll in the
opposite direction with Sherman
tanks for the combat zones.

▼ advertisement, 1943

This Pennsylvania Railroad advertisement underlined the importance of the average and unglamorous freight car to the overall war effort.

advertisement, 1944 ▼

A New York Central ad illustrating what life was like aboard a troop train.

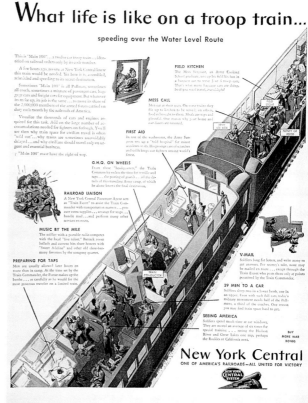

▼ poster/stamp, 1942

Union Pacific's "Give 'em Hell, Pals!" depicts a railworker directly handing a cannon shell to an infantryman still wearing World War I-style equipment.

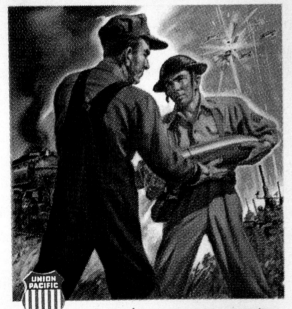

poster/stamp, 1943 ▲

This Union Pacific poster shows the importance of the railworker to the overall war effort.

poster/stamp, 1944 ▼

Under a dark, star-speckled sky, railroads working around the clock move tanks from their factory with the curious statement that "only the stars are neutral."

▲ **poster/stamp, 1943**

The most efficient way of getting a combat tank to a shipping port was via rail.

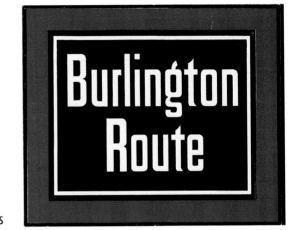

▲

baggage label, 1948
A simple but bold Burlington
Route baggage label echoed
the signage on the train itself.

For those interested in collecting images

from the railroad's Golden Age, an incredibly wide variety of material is available for every pocketbook. During the twentieth century, advertising reached its zenith, and the railroads put out tens of thousands of advertisements, most of them placed in popular magazines of the time period.

By building a collection of these advertisements, one can map an important period of social history of the United States—from the start of the century, when rail travel was still often the privilege of the wealthy, through the Roaring Twenties, the Great Depression, the Second World War, and, finally, the Fabulous Fifties, when passenger rail travel began a great and rapid decline. A collection spanning these periods also represents every important art form of the century—from Edwardian, art nouveau, and art deco to futurism and modernism.

What does it take to form a collection of railway periodical advertising art? Not much

meal check, 1944

This meal check for travel aboard the *California Zephyr* was issued to soldiers and officials traveling on government business.

▼

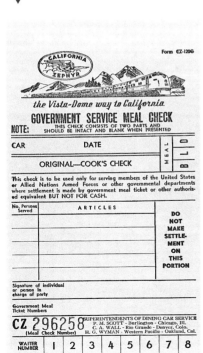

really, and that's fortunate. Virtually every town has some form of flea market or swap meet where the vintage magazines featuring these ads can be picked up for just a few dollars. Also, many paper-collectables dealers separate such advertisements by categories and, although the price of each ad may be a few dollars, the time saved by buying in this manner is significant. Rarely will these ads exceed $20, and that is for the rarest or most popular images.

Collecting rail ephemera is extremely organized and quite popular, and there are dozens of rail-enthusiast clubs across the country. It should be noted, however, that these organizations are usually much more interested in the information involved in the collectables rather than in the artwork or graphics. As an example, train schedules are prized by these collectors and prices can rapidly escalate on these items due to rarity. Schedules often featured extremely good artwork or graphics, but rail collectors are usually interested not in the art but in the information contained in the schedule. However, schedules can also be found at swap meets for just a few dollars.

Many larger cities feature regular paper-collectable shows at which all types of paper art can be found. Usually each dealer at such an event will have at least some representation of rail art or graphics available for purchase.

Another very popular form of rail collecting is railway luggage labels, and extremely interesting collections of these labels can be obtained for minimal outlay. In fact, it's fun to take a piece of vintage luggage and apply some of the less rare labels for that well-traveled look! Labels can run from a few dollars up to one hundred dollars for the rarest and most desirable examples.

Those collecting railway posters will find that prices can really start to escalate, and this is for numerous reasons. First, railway collectors who desire certain poster images may be willing to pay higher prices to acquire them. Second, art or poster collectors may not be overly interested in railroads, but they are drawn to a piece by the quality of the image or by the artist who executed it. Some rail posters can easily surpass the $10,000 mark due to the desirability of the work or the artist. A good source for this more rarefied stratum of collecting is Poster Auctions International (37 Riverside Drive, New York, New York, 10023) which holds regular poster auctions and produces extremely attractive hardbound catalogues that often feature rare or desirable railway posters.

As with any form of collecting, condition is paramount. Posters are often professionally graded by dealers along an alphabetic scale. An "A" poster indicates that the item is as close to mint as possible with no tears, discoloration, etcetera. Rarely will a reputable deal-

advertisement (detail), 1936

This marvelous piece of advertising art illustrates two of the famous *20th Century Limited* streamliners of the New York Central System.

er handle an item in the "C" category. While there can be a lot of latitude in condition for items that cost just a few dollars, on the high end collectors should not wander too far below items rated "A-." The buyer should make a thorough examination of a poster before making a purchase. It should also be noted that the most expensive or collectable posters have been mounted on linen, which acts as a preservative; the prospective purchaser should always opt for a linen-mounted piece. Also, a close look at the poster with a magnifying glass will usually reveal any flaws or repairs.

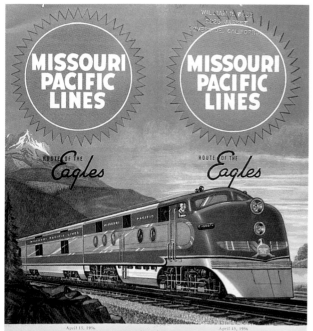

▲

timetable, 1956

Rail timetables are extremely popular with collectors.

If one decides to collect advertisements or luggage labels, nice collections can be built up in three-ring binders, with the objects placed in archival pages. Most large photographic supply stores carry a variety of clear pages divided into different size compartments into which the art can be inserted for display. Be sure to obtain pages that are clearly marked as archival since these materials do not contain harmful polyvinyl chlorides (PVCs) that will damage the art. Also, care should be taken not to glue any collected item to a page, since this essentially negates their value. Since these vintage items are often not printed on the best paper, they should not be exposed to extreme heat or sunlight, as these sources will cause damage.

Collecting rail images can be a fascinating venture into a lifestyle that, if not completely gone, has metamorphosed into something completely different.